This book belongs to:

....

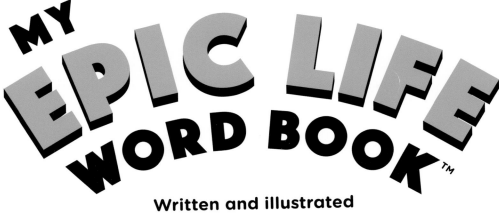

MY EPIC LIFE WORD BOOK™

Written and illustrated
by Mrs Wordsmith

"THIS IS THE WORD BOOK FOR THE 21ST CENTURY."

"This is the word book for the 21st century. I can't imagine a more delightful way to learn about words than with these wild and hilarious characters. What's especially exciting is that My Epic Life uses the very latest in the science of learning to grab children's attention and teach them words about their world. Educators take note! This book will not only improve children's vocabulary, it will accelerate it at epic speed."

SUSAN NEUMAN

Professor of Childhood Education and Literacy Development, NYU

WHAT'S INSIDE?

1,000 hilariously illustrated words to help kids with counting, shapes and measurements, hygiene, outdoor adventures, arts and crafts, social skills, and emotional awareness. These are epic words that will stretch every child's imagination, preparing them to succeed in school and life in an epic way.

EPIC WORDS FOR AN EPIC LIFE

This is not your average book. It's a book about words, but it's also a handbook for any child who wants to live a truly epic life. In this book, a cast of word-hungry animals will guide kids through everything they need to know to turn home, school, and life into a learning adventure.

This word book, illustrated by our superstar Hollywood artists, will show you that anything in life can be epic. Getting dressed in the morning? Make it epic. On your way to school? Go epic. Learning to count? Five, ten, fifteen, epic.

We designed this word book to be hilariously fun and endlessly surprising, but kids are guaranteed to learn a lot along the way. Research has proven time and again that if kids are having fun, they are in the perfect zone for deep learning. And they don't even know it!

The words in this book were curated from relevant, global curriculum lists for kids aged four to eight. But we're Mrs Wordsmith, so we added more challenging words to the mix, like **devour** and **reflect**, and some epic words, like **3D printer**. We also paired everyday words with useful, funny, or interesting collocations – or word pairs – that our data engine has identified as being worth learning.

We know that even the smallest children are capable of learning big words and accelerating their vocabulary knowledge. And big kids need to learn how to read and manipulate words they already know. So there's something here for everyone. Those who aren't reading yet may need a little help from a grown up, but confident readers can take this book to a quiet spot and get lost in it. No matter what age, we know that kids love to return to our books over and over again, whether to find the word they want or just for the fun of it.

This is a book that looks forward, not back. It gets children excited about their world today and what it might look like tomorrow, with words and illustrations focused on everything from emotions to food, hygiene to the future of technology. There will be joy. There will be tears. There will be a dog brushing his teeth on a hoverboard. Welcome to My Epic Life Word Book.

CONTENTS

GET TO KNOW YOUR WORD BOOK

WHAT'S ON THE PAGE?

Core word

Definition

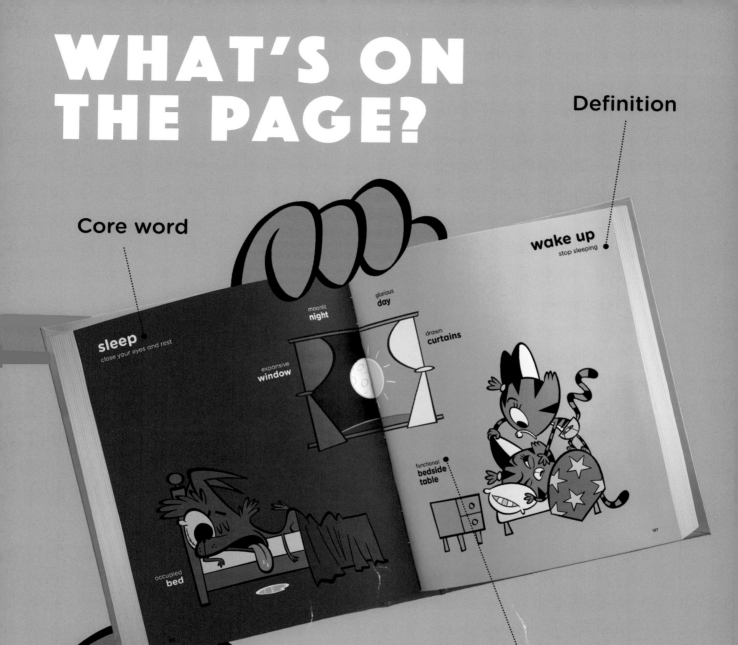

sleep
close your eyes and rest

moonlit
night

expansive
window

glorious
day

drawn
curtains

wake up
stop sleeping

functional
bedside table

occupied
bed

187

CAN YOU FIND BOGART?

Bogart the larva is often hiding inside this book. Can you find him?

WORD PAIRS

These are words that our data says commonly appear alongside each main word — and they make them even more epic!

WORD CARTOONS

We've turned some of our illustrations into mini cartoons! Turn to the back of the book to see what there is for you to watch.

QR CODE

Simply scan the QR code with the camera on your smartphone or tablet. Some devices will require a QR scanner to do this. This can be downloaded free from your app store of choice. If you have any trouble, you can find more detailed instructions at mrswordsmith.com.

adjust
p163

challenge
p200

dangerous
p181

design
p92

devour
p147

drowsy
p152

flush
p155

gargle
p51

gulp
p213

toug
p197

234

11

WORDS FOR
EPIC ME

My
Body

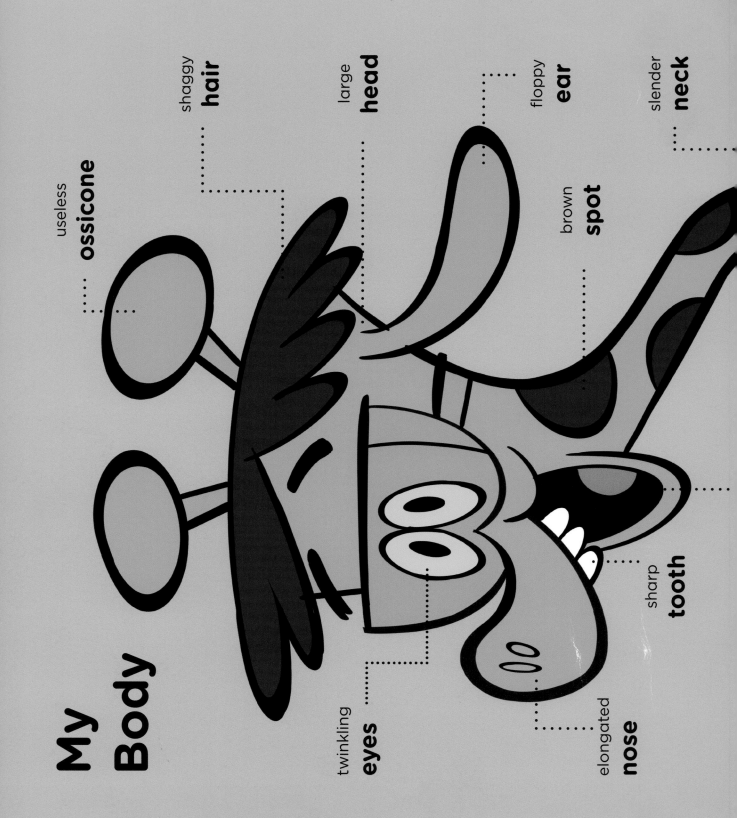

useless **ossicone**

shaggy **hair**

large **head**

floppy **ear**

slender **neck**

brown **spot**

twinkling **eyes**

sharp **tooth**

elongated **nose**

14

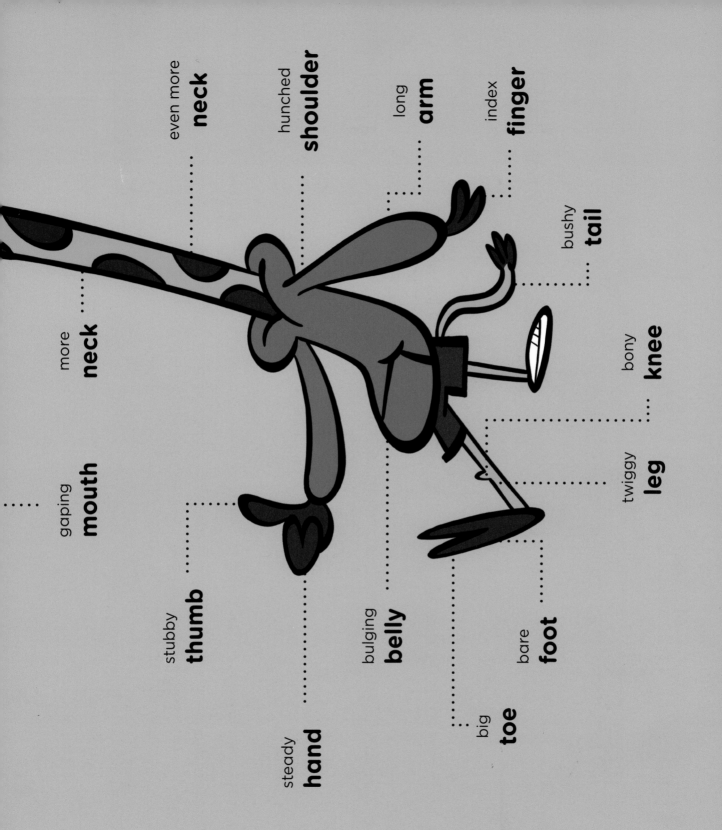

even more **neck**

hunched **shoulder**

long **arm**

index **finger**

bushy **tail**

more **neck**

bony **knee**

gaping **mouth**

twiggy **leg**

stubby **thumb**

bulging **belly**

steady **hand**

bare **foot**

big **toe**

All You Need is...

love
deep caring
and affection

unique

the only one of its kind

nonconformist

someone who doesn't do things like everyone else

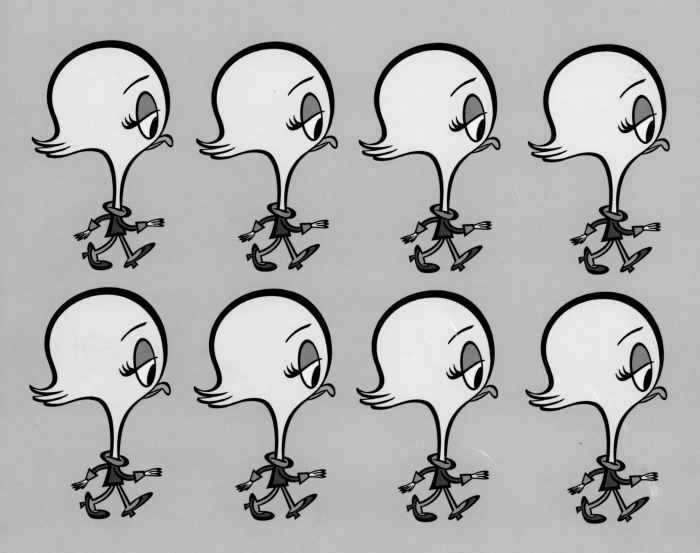

friends

people who get along well
and love each other

friendship
bracelets

adventurous
friend

true
friend

best
friends

old
friend

family
friend

new
friend

respect

treat others with appreciation and behave politely

polite
behaving in a respectful way

sob

cry noisily with loud gasps

LET IT ALL OUT

cry

get teary because you are so emotional

wail

cry out with a
long, high noise

blubber

cry uncontrollably
and loudly

comfort

soothe someone and
make them feel better

sympathetic
understanding how somebody feels
and comforting them

pity

a feeling of sadness
for someone else

relate

understand someone because
of something in common

mischievous

naughty and playful

blame

say that something
is someone's fault

forgive

stop feeling angry
with someone

playful

laughing

cheerful

happy

goofy

glum

confused

upset

angry

sad

include

let everyone join in

BEARNICE VS THE TICKLE TWINS

laughing

howling

hysterical

unable to control yourself

NOT IN THE MOOD

frown
look sad with your eyebrows pushed down

pout
stick your lips out in a moody way

scowl

frown in an angry
or bad-tempered way

sulk

be quiet and grumpy

41

bashful

shy and nervous
around others

enormous
present

rotating
disco ball

flickering
candles

lucky
birthday boy

birthday
cake

43

lucky
birthday girl

squeal
make a long,
high-pitched noise

44

festive
bunting

dangling
piñata

try

make an effort
to do something

WORDS FOR
TIME

BRUSH YOUR TEETH FOR **2** MINUTES

30 seconds

60 seconds

90 seconds

cutting-edge
hoverboard

gargle

make a funny noise as you wash your mouth and throat

minty
toothpaste

2 minutes

manual
toothbrush

DAYS OF THE WEEK

bone
Monday

basic bone broth
Friday

chickenless bone bucket
Thursday

bone burger
Tuesday

bones on toast
Wednesday

bone cone
Saturday

supersize bone
Sunday

Months of the Year

January

February

March

July

August

September

One year. No washing. No haircuts. Go!

April

May

June

October

November

December

A Worm for All Seasons

spring

summer

winter

autumn

57

The Chinese Zodiac

rat   ox   tiger

horse   goat   monkey

I was born in the Year of the...

rabbit   **dragon**   **snake**

rooster   **dog**   **pig**

WORDS FOR
NUMBERS, SHAPES, AND SIZES

impressive
really good or awesome

**five
doughnuts**

**ten
doughnuts**

**fifteen
doughnuts**

**twenty
doughnuts**

regret
feel bad and wish
you hadn't done something

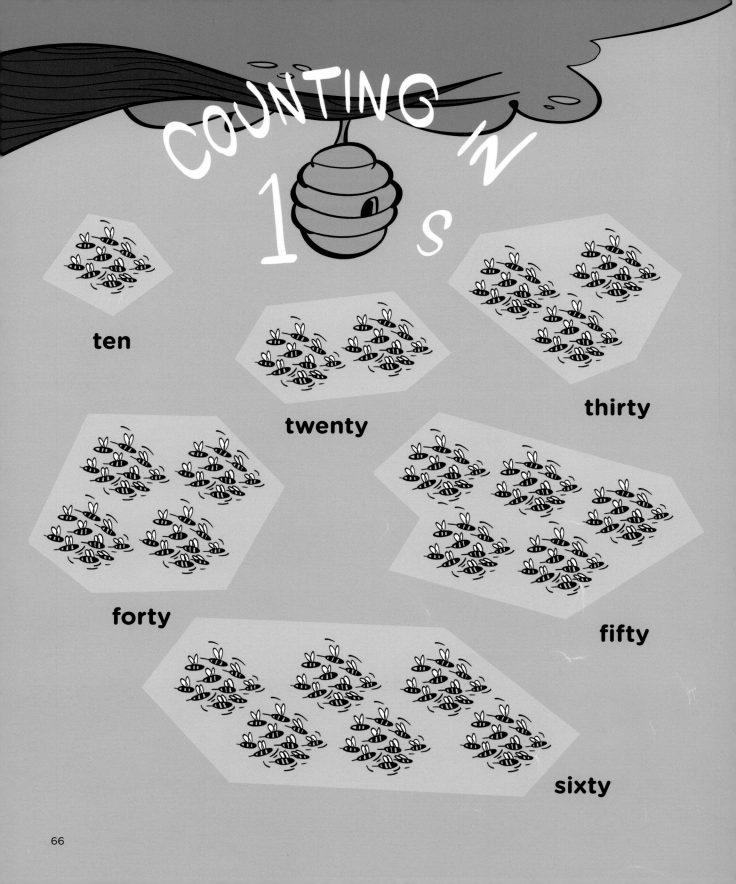

COUNTING IN 10s

ten

twenty

thirty

forty

fifty

sixty

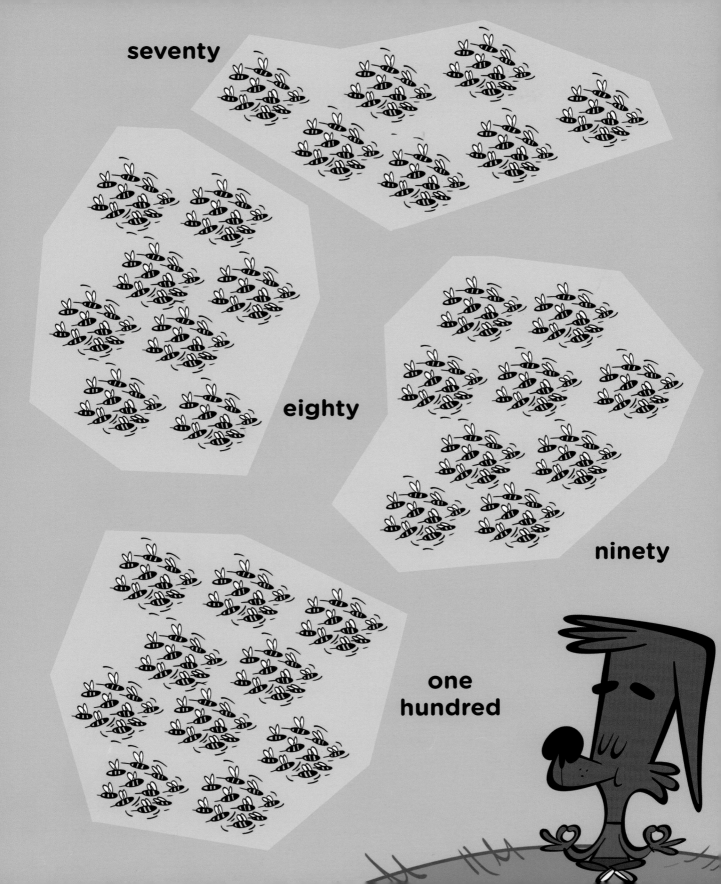

seventy

eighty

ninety

one
hundred

SHAPES

square   circle   triangle

rhombus

rectangle

star

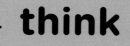
think
what your brain does all the time

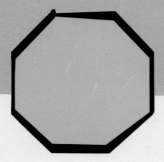

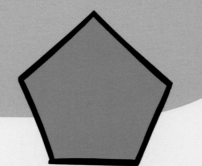

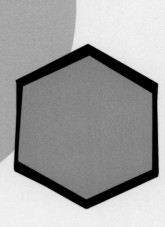
hexagon

octagon

pentagon

huge

massive

71

DON'T LOOK DOWN

soaring

· ·

high

· ·

vertigo

the dizzy feeling of losing balance when you look down from high up

towering
....

lofty
....

73

share

have or do something with other people

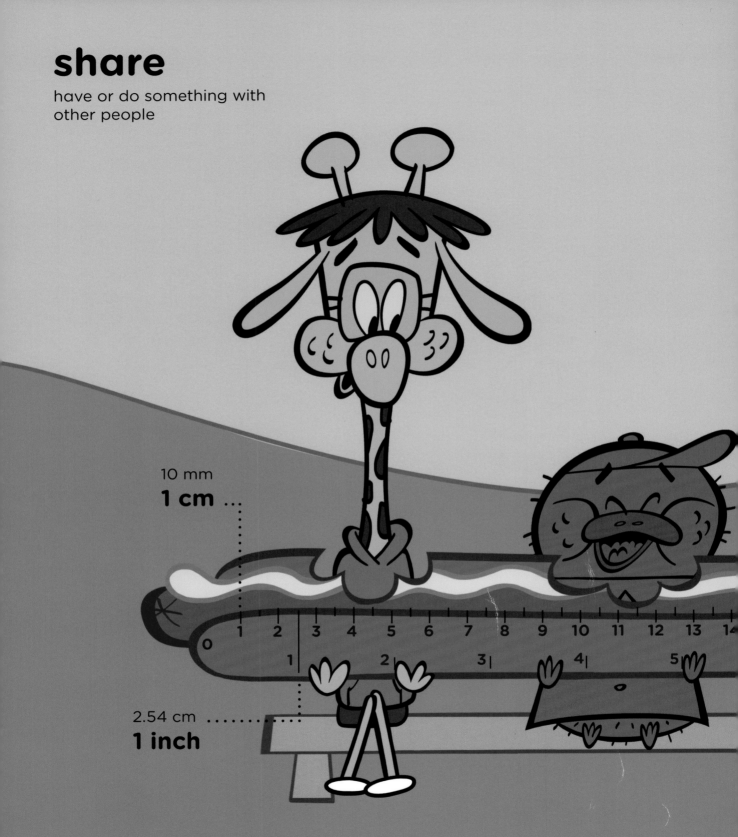

10 mm
1 cm ....

2.54 cm ....
1 inch

Foot-long Hotdog

30.48 cm
12 inches
1 foot

WORDS FOR

WHERE AND HOW

on

in

beneath

behind

in front of

next to

over

under

around

toasted
marshmallow

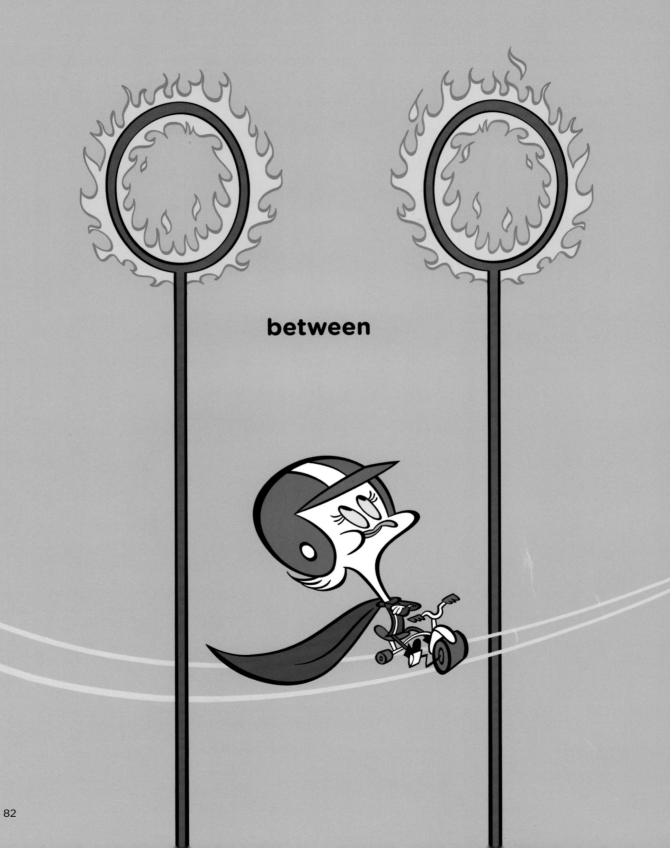

between

through

amazing
incredible or surprising

upside-down

muddled

mixed up and the wrong
way around

opposite

completely different in every way

spectacular
lightning

gloomy
clouds

heavy
raindrops

scorching
sun

wispy
clouds

golden
sunshine

WORDS FOR

MY EPIC TECHIE LIFE

DARE TO BE DIFFERENT

YOU WERE BORN TO MAKE A DIFFERENCE

BUILD YOUR OWN BEAR

need
want something that is important to you

design
plan to make something

rough
.... **sketch**

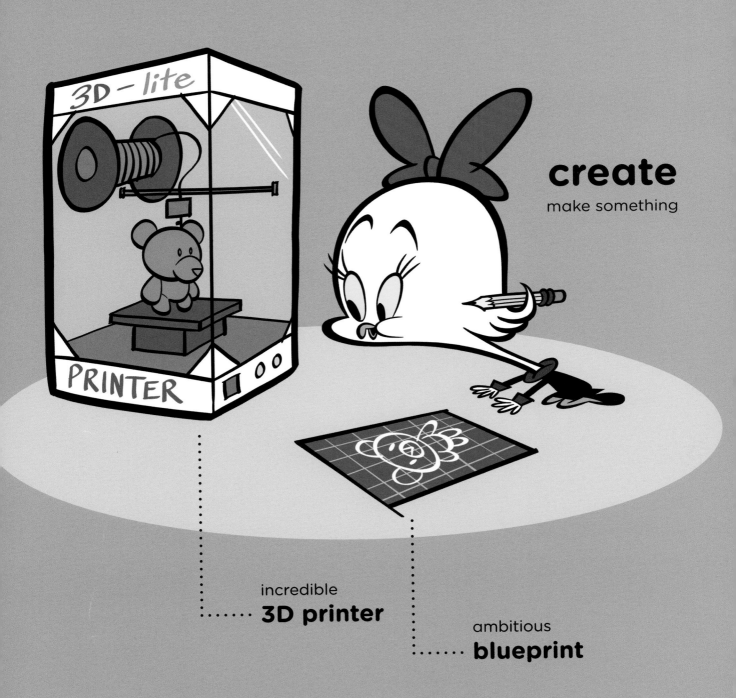

create
make something

incredible
3D printer

ambitious
blueprint

Oz's SCOOT PUP FASHION

beautiful
crystal

lightspeed
space racer

glazed
doughnut

extravagant
lobster

gourmet
burger

wear
have clothes on your body

swaggering
cowboy

complex
circuit board

fierce
tiger

steamed
bun

fried
egg

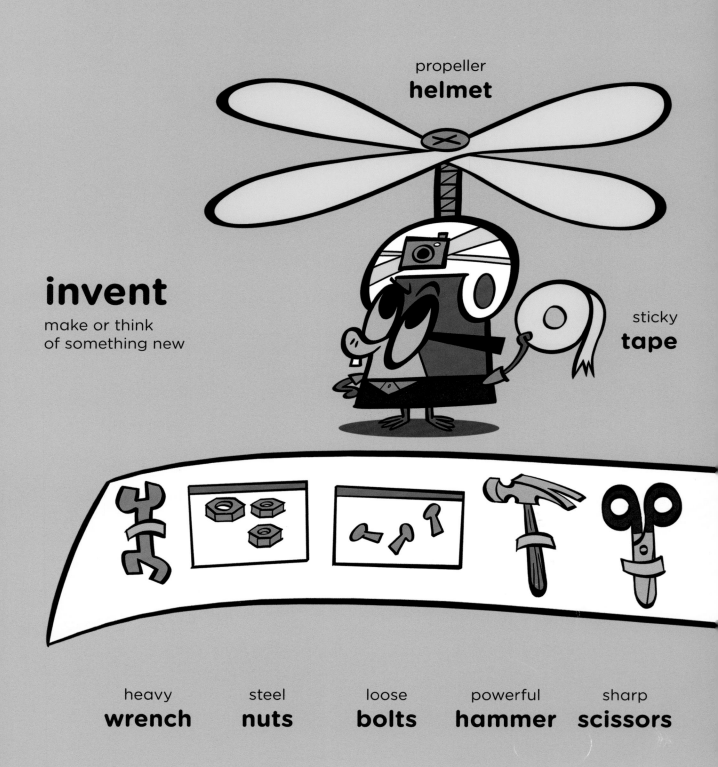

propeller
helmet

invent
make or think
of something new

sticky
tape

heavy
wrench

steel
nuts

loose
bolts

powerful
hammer

sharp
scissors

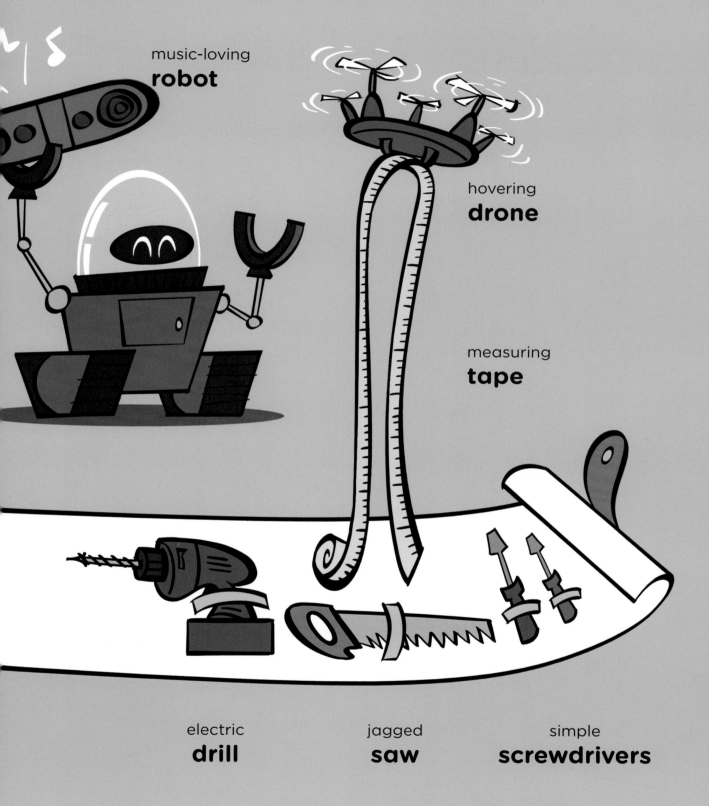

music-loving
robot

hovering
drone

measuring
tape

electric
drill

jagged
saw

simple
screwdrivers

SCOOTER WORKSHOP

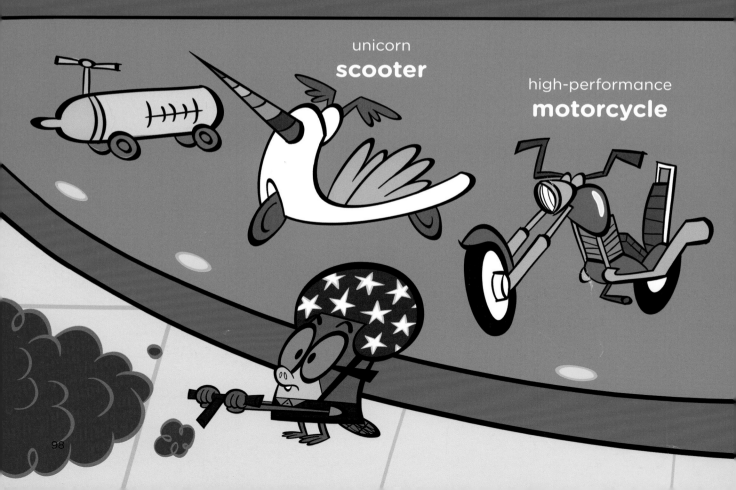

milk
scooter

unicorn
scooter

high-performance
motorcycle

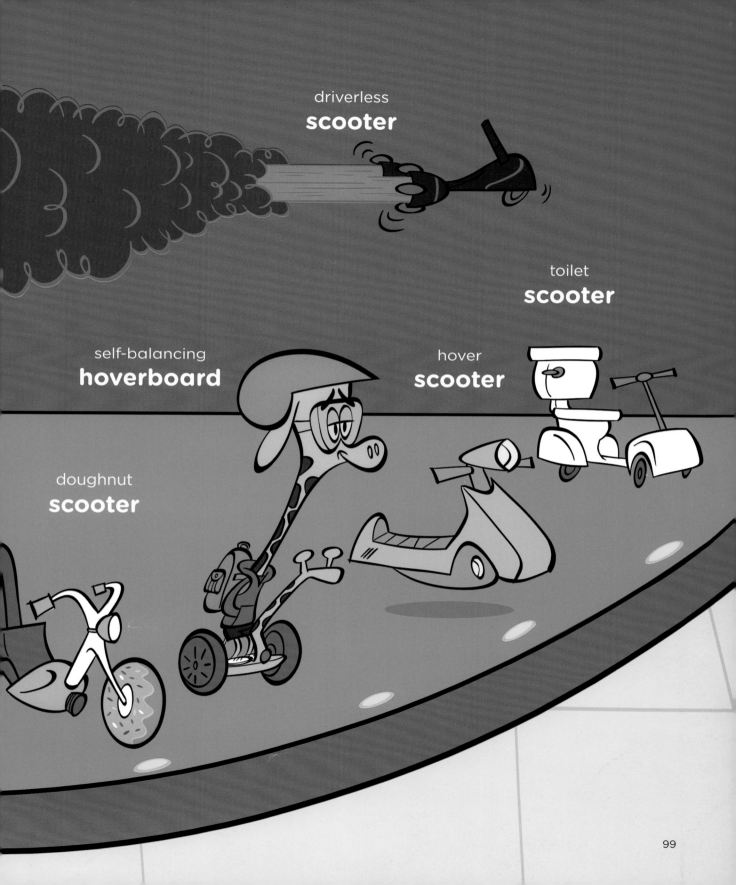

driverless
scooter

toilet
scooter

self-balancing
hoverboard

hover
scooter

doughnut
scooter

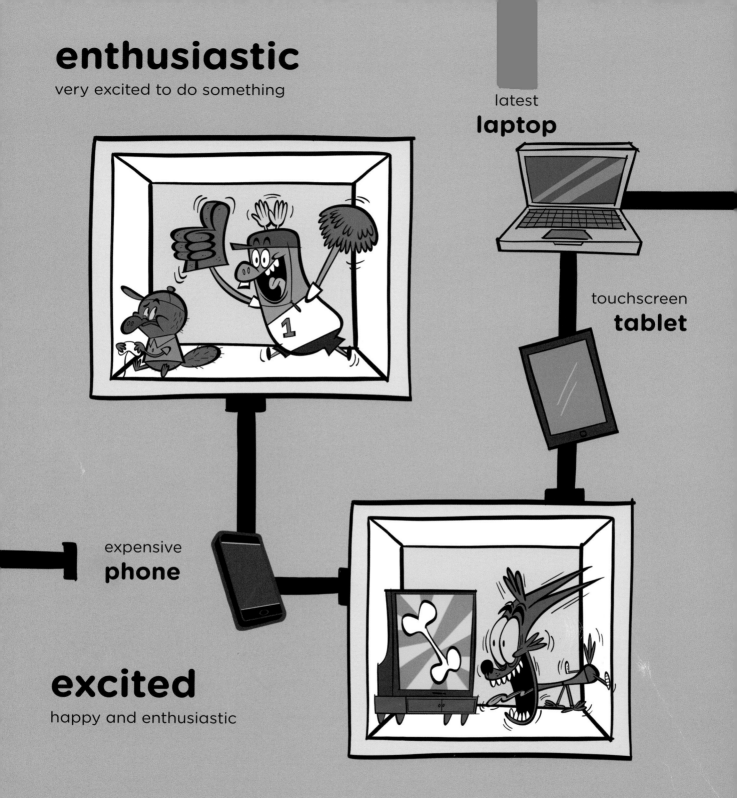

enthusiastic
very excited to do something

latest
laptop

touchscreen
tablet

expensive
phone

excited
happy and enthusiastic

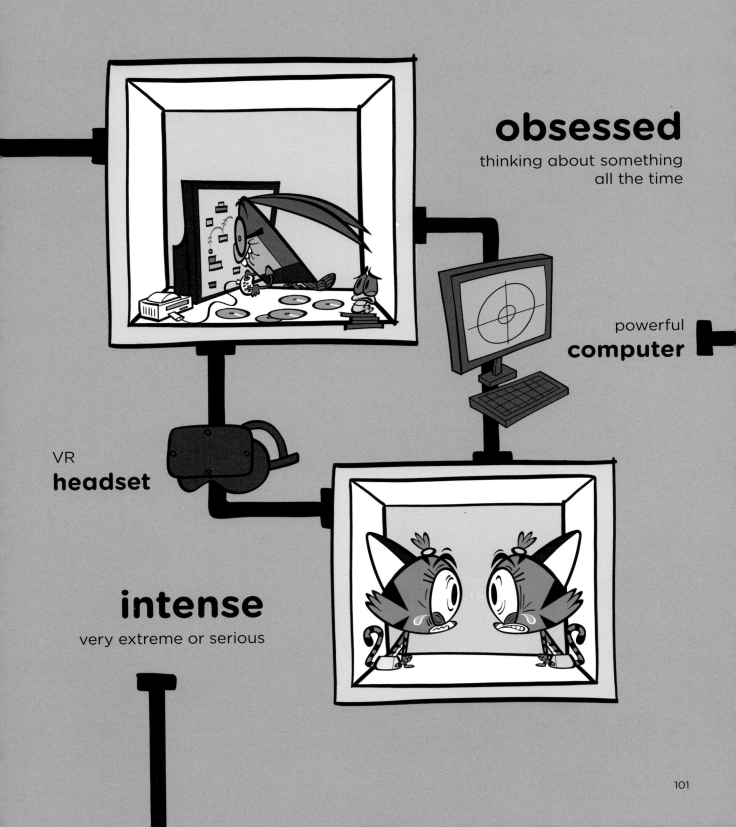

obsessed
thinking about something
all the time

powerful
computer

VR
headset

intense
very extreme or serious

HOW TO MAKE A VIDEO GAME

game designer

dreams up the video game

producer
makes sure everything
is going to plan

user interface
designer
plans how the game will look

researcher
finds information to make the game better

writer

creates the story and world of the game

concept artist

draws the world, characters,
and objects in the game

game tester
plays the game to make sure it works

programmer
writes the code to make the game work

animator

makes the game move like a cartoon

WORDS FOR
LEARNING AND CREATING

inspire

make someone excited to do something

difficult
not easy

dinosaur **puzzle**

furious
very angry or raging

tricky

needing lots of skill or practice

airborne
**juggling
clubs**

scattered
playing cards

THAT'S CHEATING, BRICK!

problem
something that you need to fix or solve

shortcut
a quicker or easier way of
doing something

solution

a way to fix or solve a problem

ARTY PARTY

paint
make a picture with paint

spotless
apron

insulted

how you feel when someone does something you find rude

wooden **easel**

taut **canvas**

121

sculpt

make shapes out
of something like
stone or clay

masterpiece
an amazing work of art

... passion
very powerful feeling

scribbled
picture

white
chalk

thick
paintbrush

waterproof
glue

moist
clay

hand-painted
mural

waxy
crayons

metallic
spray paint

spilled
glitter

125

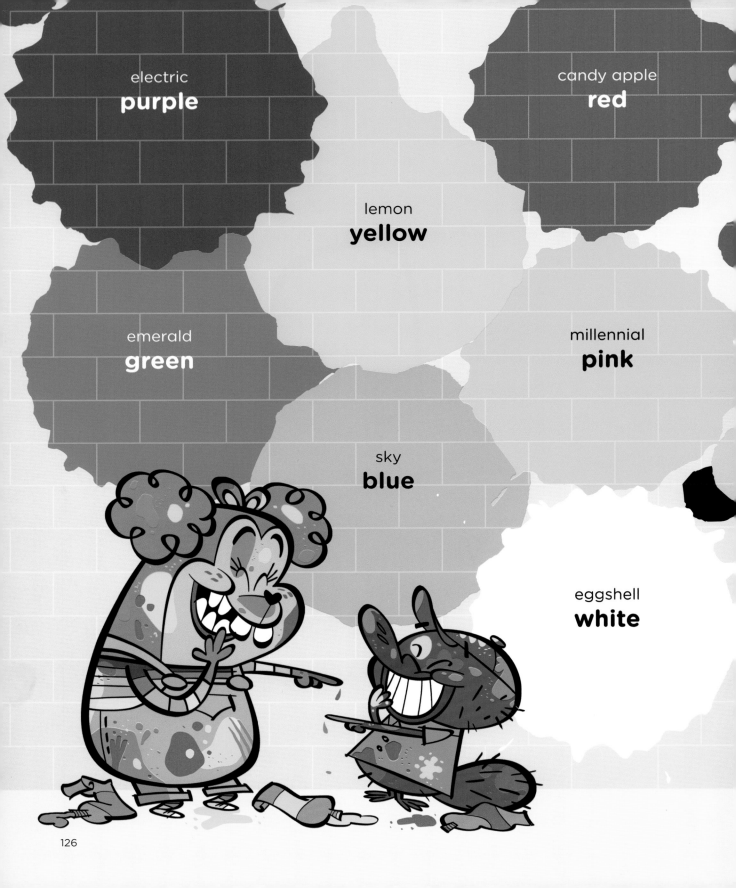

electric
purple

candy apple
red

lemon
yellow

emerald
green

millennial
pink

sky
blue

eggshell
white

126

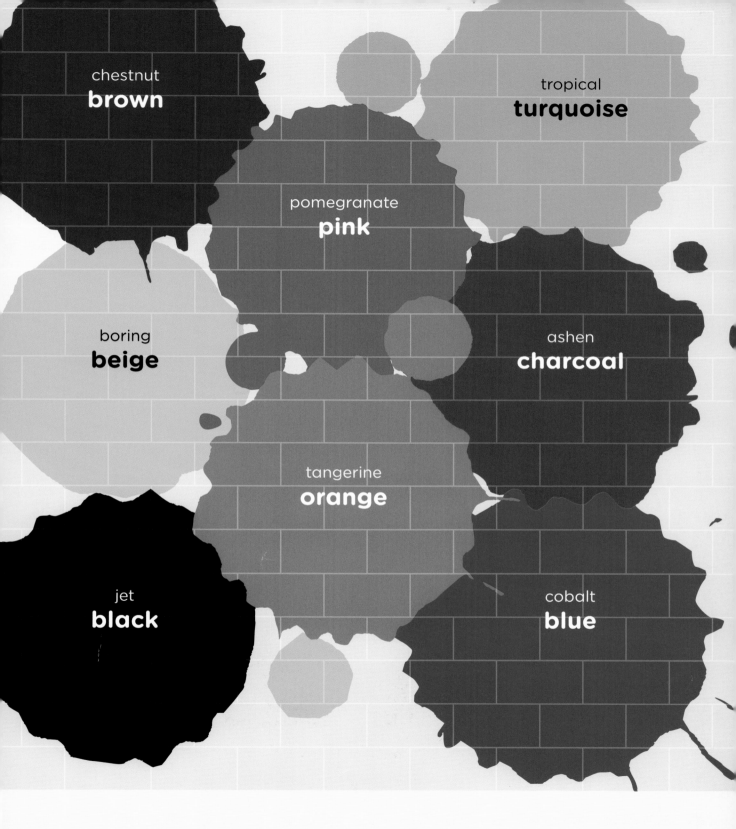

chestnut
brown

tropical
turquoise

pomegranate
pink

boring
beige

ashen
charcoal

tangerine
orange

jet
black

cobalt
blue

good

better

practice

doing something again and
again to get better at it

best

skip
move lightly on foot
with a hop and a jump

crawl
move on your
hands and knees

walk
move on foot at a normal speed

run

move quickly on foot

tangled
earphones

bulky
**pencil
case**

spiky
compass

handy
calculator

reusable
**water
bottle**

133

influence

change the way other people act

write
make words or letters

focus
think about something
without getting distracted

empower
give someone the ability
to do something

WORDS FOR

MY EPIC EVERYDAY LIFE

neat

arranged in a tidy and ordered way

sharp
knife

heatproof
spatula

wooden
spoon

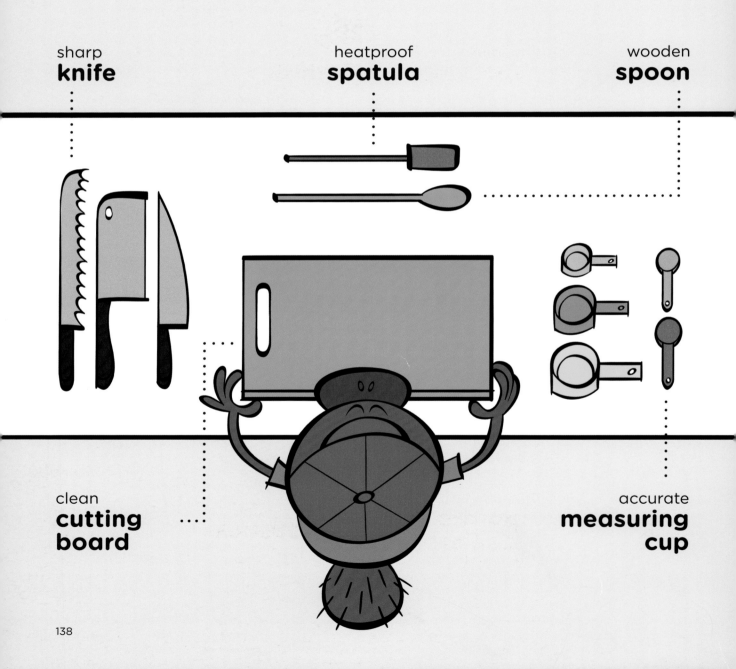

clean
**cutting
board**

accurate
**measuring
cup**

serving
spoon

metal
spatula

handheld
whisk

folded
napkin

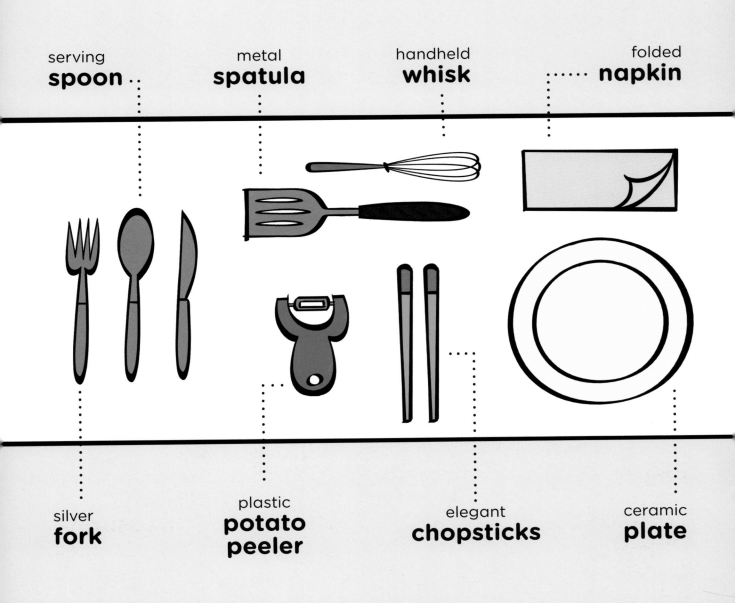

silver
fork

plastic
**potato
peeler**

elegant
chopsticks

ceramic
plate

1 large **onion**

2 raw **ginger**

3 leftover **ham**

4 free-range **chicken**

13 aromatic **herbs**

5 juicy **shrimp**

6 organic **beef**

7 creamy **butter**

8 silken **tofu**

9 crunchy **celery**

10 peppery **radish**

11 organic **carrot**

12 fresh **cabbage**

22 healthy **sweet potato**

14 spicy
curry powder

15 expensive
saffron

24 fiery
hot sauce

25 strong
vinegar

16 fluffy
quinoa

17 pungent
garlic

18 canned
tuna

26 sea
salt

27 cracked
pepper

19 white
flour

23 humble
potato

28 pure
olive oil

21 handmade
pasta

20 crusty
bread

In the mood for food?

hungry
wanting or needing food

empty
bowl

142

starving

very, very hungry

sesame
bun

steamed
broccoli

reject

strongly say no
to something

What's Cooking?

eager
really wanting to
do something

soaring
pancake

cast-iron
griddle ·····

144

non-stick
skillet

robotic
chef

sizzling
frying pan

heavy
lid

red-hot
stovetop

stainless steel
saucepan

eat
put something in your mouth and swallow it

scrumptious **pies**

stylish **dining table**

sturdy **chair**

devour
eat quickly and greedily

147

succulent
kebab

steamed
dumplings

foot-long
hotdog

PLATO'S

TACOS

wood-fired
pizza

authentic
taco

sticky
noodles

PT

PT

TACO1

healthy
salad

hand-rolled
sushi

classic
burger

Lunch
Rush

shriek
make a short, loud cry

plump
blueberry

fuzzy
kiwi

luscious
strawberry

rosy
apple

hand-picked
grape

overripe
banana

tropical
coconut

organic
pear

refreshing
watermelon

zingy
lemon

tangy
orange

that's not a
banana

awake

not sleeping

yawning

taking a big, tired breath

drowsy

tired and about
to fall asleep

catnapping
sleeping during the day

Take the Plunge!

unroll
unwind or unwrap

quilted
toilet paper

flush
empty the toilet
with water

overflowing
toilet

plastic
pipes

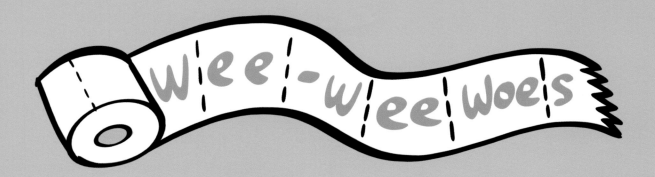

desperate

needing something very badly

secure
lock

flustered
confused and panicking

empty
roll

relief
the nice feeling when something
unpleasant stops

portable
potty

Bath Time!

bubble
bath

ecstatic

full of joy or happiness

power
shower

free-standing
bathtub

miserable
unhappy or uncomfortable

scalding　　　　　**hot**　　　　　**lukewarm**

adjust

move or change
something slightly

cold   **numbing**   **glacial**

BEAR HAIR CARE

soak
leave something in water

shampoo
wash your hair with special hair soap

perm

pin curls

crew cut

ponytail

comb-over

bun

bob

braids

mohawk

FIX UP

polish
rub something to
make it shinier

comb
get knots out of your
hair with a comb

brush
neaten your hair by running
a brush through it

apply lotion
rub cream into your skin

Dress Up

skinny **jeans**

frayed **shorts**

baggy **sweatshirt**

patterned **blouse**

oversized **scarf**

cashmere **gloves**

bowler **hat**

pom-pom **hat**

pleated **skirt**

get dressed
put clothes on

sharp **suit**

snazzy **tie**

warm **mittens**

thick **socks**

golden
crown

tilted
beret

printed
T-shirt

comfortable
hoodie

neat
uniform

leopard print
coat

wooden
geta

platform
shoes

old-fashioned
top hat

baseball
cap

party
hat

matching
tracksuit

football
jersey

puffy
jacket

summer
dress

designer
slides

cowboy
boots

Lace up

classic
high-tops

understand
know how or why
something works

golden
low-tops

high-heel
high-tops

fluffy
high-tops

winged
high-tops

wheely
mid-tops

snakeskin
mid-tops

light-up
mid-tops

platform
low-tops

metallic
low-tops

moccasin
low-tops

imagine

use your mind to see the world
completely differently

brave
knight

ferocious
dragon

STEALTH MODE

stealthy
trying not to be seen
or heard

telltale
clue

hide
cover something up
so no one sees it

inadequate
hiding place

seek
try to find

suspicious
footprints

conclusive
evidence

sloppy
careless and messy

unusual **lamp**

elegant **coffee table**

fix
put something back together again

comfortable
armchair

epic
race track

shaggy
rug

LIVING VROOOM

reckless

not caring about how
dangerous something could be

risky

possibly causing something bad to happen

tempting
button

dangerous

not safe

electrical
cable

181

HANDLE WITH CARE

magnificent **chandelier**

glass **goblet**

delicate **flute**

porcelain **vase**

reusable **glass**

FRAGILE

shatter

break into lots of little pieces

decorative
jug

sturdy
mug

vintage
teacup

cappuccino
cup

doodle

draw or scribble without
thinking about it

CHILLING OUT

unwind
relax after being busy or worried

tranquil
calm and quiet

sleep
close your eyes and rest

moonlit
night

expansive
window

occupied
bed

wake up
stop sleeping

glorious
day

drawn
curtains

functional
bedside table

dream

things you see in your mind
when you're asleep

nightmare

a scary or upsetting dream

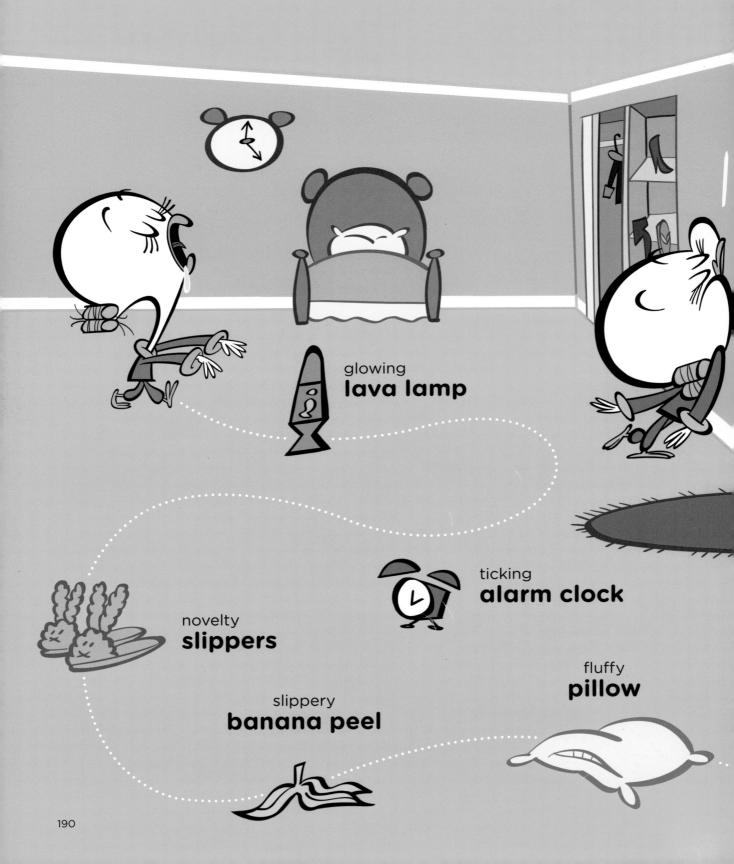

glowing
lava lamp

ticking
alarm clock

novelty
slippers

fluffy
pillow

slippery
banana peel

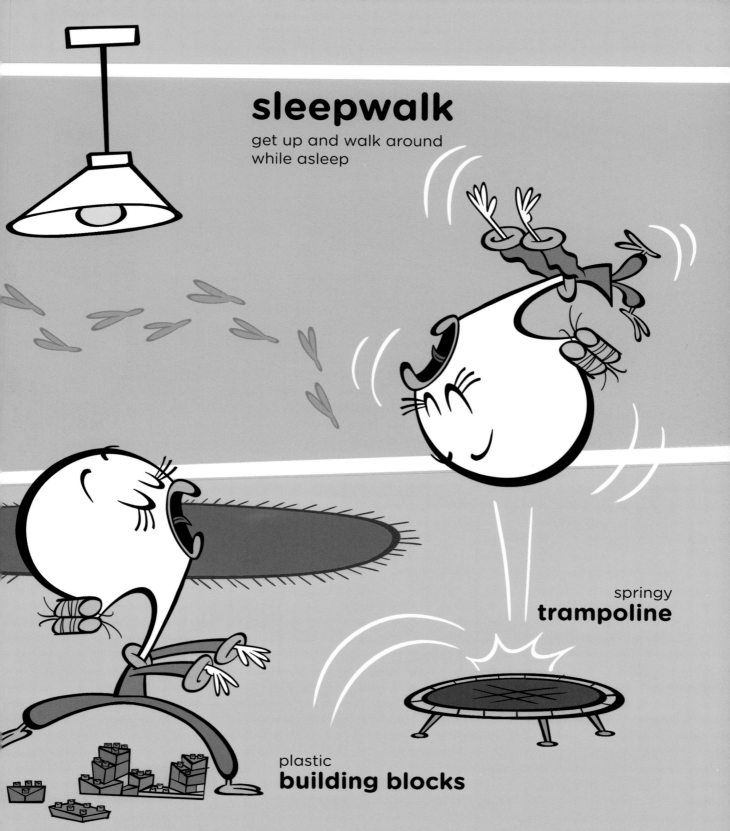

sleepwalk

get up and walk around
while asleep

springy
trampoline

plastic
building blocks

WORDS FOR
MY EPIC
OUTDOOR
ADVENTURES

SCOOTOPIA

scooter **flip**

grind **rail**

safe
free from harm or danger

protective **helmet**

steep **ramp**

upset
sad or worried
about something

long
zip wire

chase
hurry after something
and try to catch it

safety
net

198

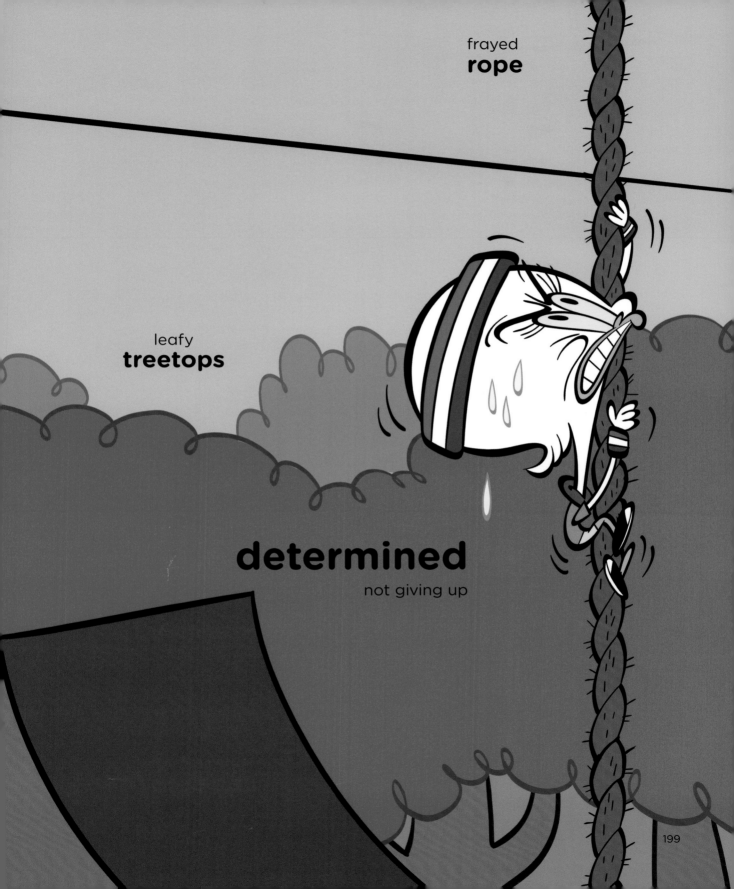

frayed
rope

leafy
treetops

determined

not giving up

199

challenge
something that is difficult
to do or finish

billowing **flags**

helpful
climbing holds

steep
climbing wall

reflection
light and images that shine back
at you in the water

reflect
think about things that
have happened

AT THE BEACH

naughty
crab

damp
beach towel

build

put things together to
make something new

fragile
seashells

majestic
sandcastle

bountiful
ice cream truck

folding
umbrella

refreshing
ice cream

striped
deck chair

bouncing
beach ball

sandy
beach

draw
create a picture
by making lines or marks

205

squawking
seagull

golden
sand

polka dot
swimsuit

protective
suntan lotion

warning
sign

leaky
snorkel

flying
kite

thermal
wetsuit

inflatable
raft

floating
life ring

calm
ocean

207

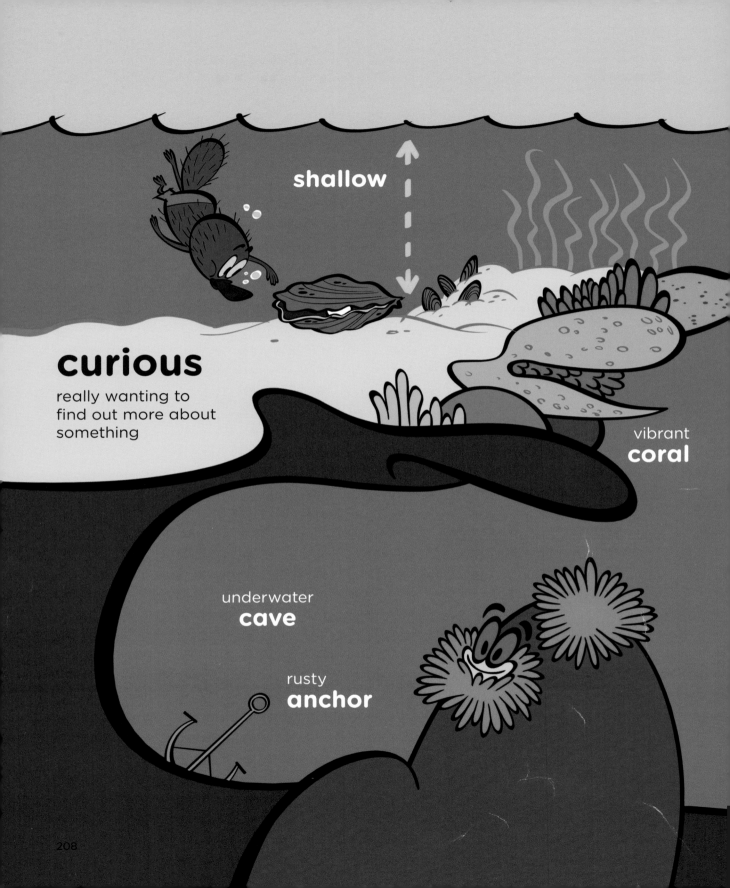

shallow

curious
really wanting to
find out more about
something

vibrant
coral

underwater
cave

rusty
anchor

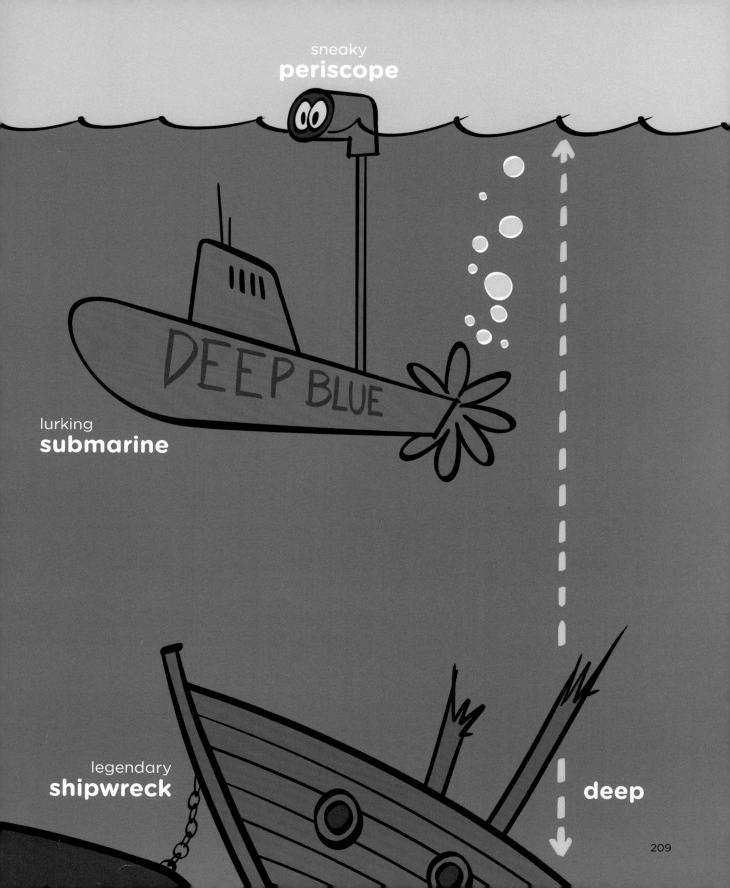

inflatable **panda**

inflatable **elephant**

inflatable **parrot**

Make a Splash!

inflatable
giraffe

shove
push someone
in a rude way

inflatable
lion

inflatable
shark

inflatable
flamingo

Paddle for your life!

anxious

worried about what might happen

inflatable
armbands

gulp
swallow a lot all at once

213

I can...

celebrate

hide

climb

extraordinary

incredible or very unusual

strawberry
cloud

elephant
cloud

bird
cloud

shark
cloud

racing car
cloud

butterfly
cloud

rabbit
cloud

daydream
imagine nice things

217

spontaneous

happening without being planned

pine
trees

overhanging
cliff

shimmering
lake

evergreen
shrub

lush
grass

218

distant
mountains

carefree
not worried about anything

naked
platypus

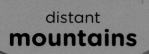

FEEL THE BURN!

exercise
move your body a lot to make it stronger

bouncy
exercise ball

persevere
keep going or carry on

concoct
make by mixing ingredients

heavy
dumbbell

compete
play against someone
or take part

THE not so GREAT OUTDOORS

bare **branch**

spooked
surprised by something
that scares you

harmless
spider

dense
underarowth

nocturnal **creatures**

huddle
crowd closely together
with other people

crackling
campfire

try

make an effort to do something

fail

try to do something and get it wrong

succeed

do well or achieve your goal

epic
fail

225

GOOD, CLEAN FUN

muddy
covered in mud

muddy **puddle**

muddy **laundry**

muddy **splash**

227

filthy
disgustingly dirty or mucky

half-eaten
pizza

vinyl
record

bulky
stereo

landline
phone

awesome

amazing or incredible

WORD CARTOONS

adjust
p163

challenge
p200

dangerous
p181

design
p92

devour
p147

drowsy
p152

flush
p155

gargle
p51

gulp
p213

hysterical
p39

imagine
p174

impressive
p62

inspire
p114

opposite
p86

starving
p143

tough
p197

try
p46

unroll
p154

INDEX

luscious,
    see **strawberry**, 150

lush,
    see **grass**, 218

M

magnificent,
    see **chandelier**, 182

majestic,
    see **sandcastle**, 204

manual,
    see **toothbrush**, 51

map, 113

March, 54

marshmallow, 81

massive, 71

masterpiece, 123

matching,
    see **tracksuit**, 171

May, 55

measuring,
    see **tape**, 97

measuring cup, 138

mechanical,
    see **brush**, 161

metal,
    see **spatula**, 139

metallic,
    see **spray paint**, 125
    see **low-tops**, 173

mid-tops, 173

milk,
    see **scooter**, 98

millennial,
    see **pink**, 126

minds, 113

minty,
    see **toothpaste**, 51

minuscule, 70

minutes, 51

mischievous, 32

miserable, 159

mittens, 169

moccasin,
    see **low-tops**, 173

mohawk, 165

moist,
    see **clay**, 124

Monday, 52

monkey, 58

moonlit,
    see **night**, 186

motorcycle, 98

mountains, 219

mouth, 15

muddled, 85

muddy, 226
    see **laundry**, 227
    see **puddle**, 226
    see **splash**, 227

mug, 146, 183

mural, 125

music-loving,
    see **robot**, 97

N

naked,
    see **platypus**, 219

napkin, 139

naughty,
    see **crab**, 204

neat, 138
    see **uniform**, 170

neck, 14

need, 92

net, 198

new,
    see **friend**, 23

newspaper, 113

next to, 79

nibble, 146

night, 186

nightmare, 189

ninety, 67

nocturnal,
    see **creatures**, 223

non-stick,
    see **skillet**, 145

nonconformist, 20

noodles, 148

nose, 14

novel, 112

novelty,
    see **slippers**, 190

November, 55

numbing, 163

nuts, 96

O

obsessed, 101

occupied,
    see **bed**, 186

ocean, 207

octagon, 69

October, 55

old,
    see **friend**, 23

old-fashioned,
    see **top hat**, 47

olive oil, 141

on, 78

one hundred, 67

onion, 140

opposite, 86

orange, 127, 151

organic,
    see **beef**, 140
    see **carrot**, 140
    see **pear**, 151

ossicone, 14

over, 80

overflowing,
    see **toilet**, 155

overhanging,
    see **cliff**, 218

overripe,
    see **banana**, 151

oversized,
    see **scarf**, 168

ox, 58

reject, 143

relate, 31

relief, 157

researcher, 105

respect, 24

reusable,
    see glass, 182

rhombus, 69

right-way-up, 85

rinse, 160

risky, 181

robot, 97

robotic,
    see chef, 145

roll, 157

rooster, 59

rope, 199

rosy,
    see apple, 151

rotating,
    see disco ball, 43

rough,
    see sketch, 92

rug, 179

run, 131

rusty,
    see anchor, 208

S

sad, 35

safe, 194

safety,
    see net, 198

saffron, 141

salad, 149

salt, 141

sand, 206

sandcastle, 204

sandy,
    see beach, 205

Saturday, 53

saucepan, 145

saw, 97

scalding, 162

scarf, 168

scattered,
    see playing cards, 117

scissors, 96

scooter, 98, 99
    see flip, 194

scorching,
    see sun, 87

scowl, 41

screwdrivers, 97

scribbled,
    see picture, 124

scrub, 161

scrumptious,
    see pies, 147

sculpt, 122

sea,
    see salt, 141

seagull, 206

seashells, 204

seconds, 50

secure,
    see lock, 156

seek, 177

self-balancing,
    see hoverboard, 99

September, 54

serving,
    see spoon, 139

sesame,
    see bun, 143

seventy, 67

shaggy,
    see rug, 179

shallow, 208

shampoo, 164

share, 74

shark, 211
    see cloud, 216

sharp,
    see knife, 138
    see scissors, 96
    see suit, 169
    see tooth, 14

shatter, 183

shimmering,
    see lake, 218

shipwreck, 209

shoes, 170

shortcut, 118

shorts, 168

shoulder, 15

shove, 211

shower, 160

shower head, 159

shriek, 149

shrimp, 140

shrub, 218

sign, 206

silken,
    see tofu, 140

silver,
    see fork, 139

simple,
    see screwdriver, 97

sixty, 66

sizzling,
    see frying pan, 145

sketch, 92

skillet, 145

skinny,
    see jeans, 168

skip, 130

skirt, 169

sky,
    see blue, 126

sleep, 186

sleepwalk, 191

slender,
    see neck, 14

slides, 171

slippers, 190

slippery,
    see banana peel, 190

sloppy, 178

small, 70

snake, 59

snakeskin,
    see mid-tops, 173

THE EPIC TEAM BEHIND THE SCENES

Editor-in-Chief
Sofia Fenichell

Art Director
Craig Kellman

Artists

Aghnia Mardiyah
Brett Coulson

Daniel Permutt
Joan Varitek

Nicolò Mereu
Phillip Mamuyac

Writers
Tatiana Barnes
Mark Holland

Researcher
Eleni Savva

Lexicographer
Ian Brookes

Designers

Suzanne Bullat
Fabrice Gourdel

Holly Jones

James Sales
Lady San Pedro

Machine Learning
Benjamin Pettit
Stanislaw Pstrokonski

Academic Advisors
Emma Madden
Prof. Susan Neuman

Producers
Eva Schumacher Payne
Leon Welters

WORD DIFFICULTY LEVELS

At Mrs Wordsmith, we've used data science to develop a difficulty level system for vocabulary. Lots of things can make a word challenging. Some words are hard to learn because they are very long or they have unusual spellings. Others are hard to learn because they are rare or their meaning is difficult to understand.

Our difficulty levels take all of these factors into account, and support children all the way from building reading skills with sight words and phonics to developing a rich, varied vocabulary for creative and academic writing.

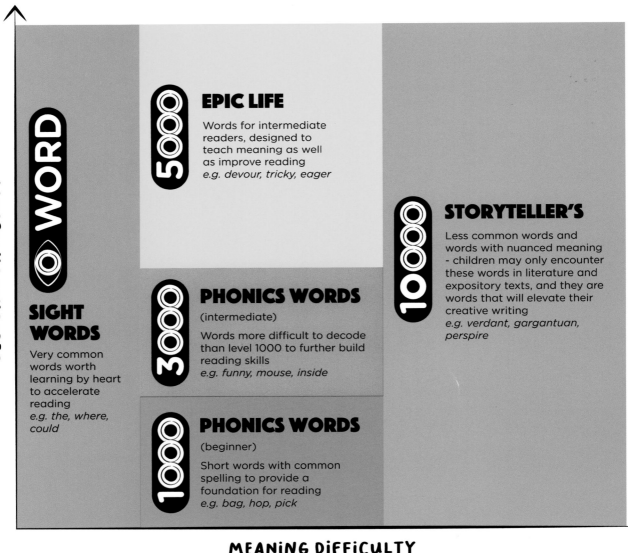

DECODING DIFFICULTY

WORD

5000 EPIC LIFE
Words for intermediate readers, designed to teach meaning as well as improve reading
e.g. devour, tricky, eager

STORYTELLER'S
Less common words and words with nuanced meaning - children may only encounter these words in literature and expository texts, and they are words that will elevate their creative writing
e.g. verdant, gargantuan, perspire

SIGHT WORDS
Very common words worth learning by heart to accelerate reading
e.g. the, where, could

3000 PHONICS WORDS
(intermediate)
Words more difficult to decode than level 1000 to further build reading skills
e.g. funny, mouse, inside

1000 PHONICS WORDS
(beginner)
Short words with common spelling to provide a foundation for reading
e.g. bag, hop, pick

MEANING DIFFICULTY